Tazio Secchiaroli
Fellini 8½

Tazio Secchiaroli
Fellini 8½

Edited by
Herausgegeben von

Diego Mormorio

teNeues

Original book title:
Tazio Secchiaroli, Fellini 8 1/2

English translation: Mila Dau, New York
English editing: Umbrage Editions, New York
German translation: Dr. Bruno Lill, Cologne
German editing and production:
Christiane Blass, Cologne

The texts included in the photographic sequence are taken from the screenplay of the movie.

ISBN 3-8238-0540-1
Printed in Italy

Abandonment and Rediscovery

I knew from the very beginning that this was a movie
meant to be seen and felt with total abandon . . .
To know nothing about the movie
and yet to abandon oneself completely to it
seems to me the perfect way to absorb this kind of story.

Federico Fellini

Hingabe und Entdeckung

Ich wußte von Anfang an, daß man diesen Film sehen
und mit größtmöglicher Hingabe fühlen mußte ...
Nichts von diesem Film zu wissen und sich in ihm vollständig
zu verlieren: dies scheint mir die kongenialste Rezeption
dieser Art von Erzählung zu sein.

Federico Fellini

At a "Public Confession" that took place in the auditorium of the Centro Sperimentale di Cinematografia (Experimental Film Center) in March 1963, a student actress questioned Fellini about some critics' charge that *8 ½* was too autobiographical. Fellini responded, "It is a bit difficult for me to set precise boundaries for *8 ½*, I mean, to determine where personal facts begin and end and where the depiction of a character (or the description of my image in so far as it becomes a character) begins. It is a distinction that I am not interested in making, that I do not want to make, and that I do not even see a need for making. I do not know what to say when I am accused of being autobiographical. I only know that it was my intention to speak of the life of a filmmaker who found himself in a spiritual tight spot, in a state of confusion. Who else could I speak of? I think it is obvious that in dealing with a theme like this—I mean this with the most sincere and abandoned confusion—that the more autobiographical the film is, the more objective it becomes. So I haven't even been able to fully grasp the meaning of this accusation, to understand if it either restricts or defines the limits of the work. I have not been able to grasp the way this accusation was intended, given the fact that the movie was simply a sincere—a most sincere—confession, with the touch of artifice and noble decep-

Im März 1963 während einer „öffentlichen Beichte" in einem Saal des Centro Sperimentale di Cinematografia, der berühmten Filmhochschule in der Nähe von Cinecittà, sagte Fellini auf die Nachfrage einer Schauspielschülerin bezüglich der Bemerkung einiger Kritiker, der Film wäre zu autobiographisch: „Es ist ein wenig schwierig für mich bei *8 ½* die genaue Grenze zu ziehen, d. h. zu definieren, wo die persönliche Geschichte anfängt bzw. endet und wo das Porträt eines Typus, die formalisierte Beschreibung eines Bildes von mir, beginnt. Diese Unterscheidung interessiert mich nicht, ich möchte sie nicht vornehmen und sehe darin auch keinen Nutzen. Auf den Vorwurf, biographisch zu sein, weiß ich nichts zu erwidern. Ich weiß nur, daß ich vorhatte, vom Leben eines Regisseurs zu berichten, der sich in geistigen Verwicklungen, in einer Art Verwirrung befindet. Von wem sollte ich da schon sprechen? Es ist klar, daß ich bei einem solchen Thema, bei der aufrichtigsten, einsamsten Verwirrung, den absolut autobiographischen Film für den objektivsten halte. So ist es mir nicht einmal gelungen, die Bedeutung des Vorwurfs richtig zu begreifen: verringern sich nun die Grenzen des Films oder präzisieren sie sich? Ich konnte den Sinn nicht verstehen, zumal der Film eine aufrichtige, nein, eine zutiefst aufrichtige Beichte war, wenn auch mit jener Finesse ausgestattet, mit jenen edlen Tricks, die ein Mensch, der anderen etwas zu erzählen hat, notwendigerweise anwenden muß, um zu kommunizieren."[1]

tion that a man who puts himself in a position confronting others to tell a story must employ in order to communicate."[1]

It was an extremely sincere confession that Fellini had considered even before he made *La Dolce Vita:* "For some time, ever since *Le notti di Cabiria,* I believe, I had wanted to make a multidimensional portrait of a man, to do a story in which diverse moments were configured. In other words, a story that took place both at the level of the reality of dreams and at the level of the reality of the imagination, with time—present, past, and future—overlapping continuously. A story with a certain contemporaneity. But I couldn't find either the story or the character. At first, I wanted him to be a lawyer, but the truth is I know very little about lawyers. And even when the story took the shape it took in *8 ½*, I had doubts about the main character to the very end. I really thought there was no need for a precise identity, because whatever the profession was, I basically wanted to tell the story of a man, the story of a soul in crisis. Something extremely objective. And it is precisely because of this need for objectivity that, paradoxically enough, I decided in the end to overcome all modesty, all shyness, and do what had seemed for some time to be the ideal solution: to talk about a film director, about someone who could have been me."[2]

There is no doubt that Fellini had conceived of the idea for *8 ½* some time before *La Dolce Vita* (which was released in 1960). We can certainly argue, however, that based on what we now know of *8 ½*, it could only have followed. Fellini could not have made his masterpiece before he met Ernst Bernhard, which only occurred after *La Dolce Vita* was released.

The first person to mention the name of the great student of Carl Gustav Jung to Fellini was the documentary filmmaker Vittorio De Seta. De Seta had tried to have his movie, *Banditi a Orgosolo*, produced by the Federiz, a short-lived production company created by Fellini and Rizzoli in 1960 which dissolved without having made a single movie. When De Seta came to the offices of Via della Croce in Rome it was, to use Tullio Kezich's words, "as a messenger of fate."[3]

"The phone number that De Seta had given him

Eine ganz aufrichtige Beichte also, an die Fellini nach eigener Aussage schon vor *La Dolce Vita* gedacht hatte: „Ich hatte schon länger vor, ich glaube sofort nach *Le notti di Cabiria* (Die Nächte der Cabiria), ein mehrdimensionales Porträt einer Person zu entwerfen, eine Geschichte zu entwickeln, in der verschiedene Augenblicke Gestalt annehmen, die sich gleichzeitig auf der Ebene der Traum-Wirklichkeit und auf der Ebene der Imaginations-Wirklichkeit abspielt und sich durch die ständige zeitliche Überbrückung von Vergangenheit, Gegenwart und Zukunft, also durch eine gewisse Gleichzeitigkeit auszeichnet. Ich fand aber nicht die richtige Erzählung, noch fand ich die richtige Person. Zunächst wollte ich einen Rechtsanwalt nehmen, aber offengestanden weiß ich fast nichts von Rechtsanwälten und so, wie sich die Geschichte in *8 ½* dann dargestellt hat, hatte ich bis zuletzt Zweifel bezüglich der Hauptfigur. Tatsächlich dachte ich nicht, daß eine bestimmte, präzise Identität notwendig sein würde, weil ich im Grunde die Geschichte eines Menschen, mit welchem Beruf auch immer, die Geschichte einer Seele in der Krise erzählen wollte. Also eine extrem objektive Angelegenheit. Und genau aus diesem Anspruch der Objektivität – auch wenn es paradox erscheint – habe ich am Ende beschlossen, jede Art von Scham, von Zurückhaltung zu überwinden und das zu machen, was mir, alles in allem, schon seit langem als die ideale Lösung erschien, nämlich von einem Regisseur zu sprechen, mit anderen Worten von jemandem wie mir selbst."[2]

Es gibt keinen Grund, daran zu zweifeln, daß Fellini die Idee zu diesem Film noch vor *La Dolce Vita* gehabt hat, der bekanntlich 1960 in die Kinos kam. Wir können aber auch mit Bestimmtheit sagen, daß *8 ½*, so wie wir ihn kennen, nur danach entstehen konnte. Um genau zu sein, hätte Fellini sein Meisterwerk nicht vor der Begegnung mit Ernst Bernhard realisieren können, und die fand erst statt, nachdem *La Dolce Vita* angelaufen war. Von Bernhard, dem großen Schüler Carl Gustav Jungs, hörte Fellini zum ersten Mal durch den Dokumentarfilmer Vittorio De Seta, welcher seinen Film *Banditi a Orgosolo* von der Federiz hatte produzieren lassen wollen. Dies war die Produktionsgesellschaft, die Fellini und Rizzoli 1960 gegründet hatten und die schon nach wenigen Monaten wieder aufgelöst wurde, ohne je einen Film produziert zu haben. Dieser Umstand brachte De Seta, wie Tullio Kezich sagte, „in der Gestalt eines Schicksalsboten"[3] in die Büros der Via della Croce in Rom.

remained in Federico's pockets for a long time, until one day he decided to dial it, thinking that he was calling a woman named Maria (a name that could very well offer mythographers an opportunity to run riot with variations on the theme of the heavenly and more-or-less mediterranean mother). But instead of Maria it was Ernst Bernhard who answered, not at all surprised by the phone call and fascinating from the very first lines he uttered."[4] This is how the relationship between Federico Fellini and the guide who was to help him "walk through the labyrinth of his soul"[5] began.

Arguably one of the great figures of this century, Bernhard was born in Berlin in 1896 of Jewish parents. In an apparently irrational move, he and his wife, Dora, had taken refuge in Rome in 1936. The move was precipitated by a dream Bernhard had on the night of October 11, 1935, which neither he nor Jung had been able to interpret: "I was in a deep underground cavern and I tried to reach the surface by climbing a narrow, steep and muddy path. [. . .] Suddenly a platoon of enemy soldiers crossed the cavern. I turned to the last soldier, an Italian with the features of an Indian, and I asked him if he had anything for me to eat. I told him that I had had nothing for three days and three nights. From his jacket pocket he took out a piece of bread and offered it to me. I asked him if by any chance he had any milk—that I'd prefer it. From the inside pocket of his jacket he took out a little bottle of milk, offered it to me, and I drank it."[6]

Bernhard would understand the meaning of his dream only later. Because of the Fascist racial laws, the scholar was interned in a camp in Calabria in 1940. But thanks to the intercession of Giuseppe Tucci, a great Orientalist scholar who held a chair in Religion and Philosophy of India and the Far East (and who was writing his *The Theory and Practice of Mandalas* at the time), Bernhard was able to return to his Roman home.

Commenting on this dream a few months before his death, Bernhard said: "I had tried in vain to help my parents, who had fled to Paris, but I could do nothing from my hideout in Rome or from the internment camp. The idea that my mother could have thought I had forgotten her was extremely painful for me. She had had no news of me. My

„Die Telefonnummer, die ihm De Seta gegeben hatte, blieb lange Zeit in der Tasche von Federico, bis er sich eines Tages entschied, die Nummer zu wählen, wohl in dem Glauben, sie sei von einer gewissen Maria, ein Name, über den sich der Mythenforscher mit Variationen über die mehr oder weniger mediterrane himmlische Mutter auslassen könnte. Statt Maria meldete sich Ernst Bernhard, der sich über das von Anfang an faszinierende Gespräch keineswegs wunderte."[4] So begann die Beziehung zwischen Federico Fellini und dem Führer, der ihm geholfen hat, „die Labyrinthe seiner Seele zu durchlaufen".[5]

Bernhard, eine der faszinierendsten Persönlichkeiten dieses Jahrhunderts, wurde 1896 in Berlin als Sohn jüdischer Eltern geboren. 1936 floh er zusammen mit seiner Frau Dora nach Rom, was aus heutiger Sicht vielleicht unvernünftig scheint, damals aber durchaus üblich war. Diesem Umzug ging in der Nacht des 11. Oktober 1935 ein Traum voraus, den weder er noch Jung verstanden hatten: „Ich befinde mich in einer tiefen Höhle unter der Erde und möchte die Oberfläche erreichen, zu der ein enger, steiler, schlammiger Weg führt. [...] Plötzlich durchquert ein Trupp feindlicher Soldaten die Höhle. Ich wende mich an den letzten dieser Soldaten, einen Italiener, allerdings mit indischen Gesichtszügen. Ich frage ihn, ob er etwas für mich zu essen hat, da ich seit drei Tagen und Nächten nichts bekommen habe. Er zieht aus seiner Jackentasche ein Stück Brot und bietet es mir an. Ich frage ihn, ob er vielleicht auch ein wenig Milch hat. Und tatsächlich holt er aus der Innentasche seiner Jacke eine kleine Flasche und reicht sie mir. Ich trinke."[6]

Den Sinn dieses Traums verstand Bernhard erst später. Auf Grundlage der faschistischen Rassengesetze wurde der Wissenschaftler 1940 in ein Lager in Kalabrien interniert. Bernhard konnte nur auf Intervention des berühmten Orientalisten Giuseppe Tucci, Professor für indische und fernöstliche Religionen und Philosophie, der in jenen Jahren sein Buch *Geheimnis des Mandala* schrieb, in sein römisches Haus zurückkehren.

Wenige Monate vor seinem Tod erläuterte Bernhard diesen Traum: „Ich habe vergeblich versucht, meinen nach Paris geflüchteten Eltern zu helfen, ich konnte aber aus meinem Versteck in Rom und aus dem Internierungslager heraus nichts für sie tun. Es war ein großer Schmerz für mich, daß meine Mutter glaubte, ich hätte sie vergessen. Sie wußte nichts von mir. Mein Vater wurde nach Polen deportiert und starb in der Gas-father was deported to Poland and died in the gas chambers; in her misery, my mother killed herself in Paris. The fact that I was not taken from the camp and deported to Poland, but instead released to return to my home, to live in hiding, was due to the famous Italian Indian scholar Tucci, who had heard of me from some patients and had obtained my freedom. The dream had said it very clearly: an Italian with an Indian face."[7]

After the war, Bernhard returned to his psychotherapeutic practice, gathering around him a group of scholars, including Emilio Servadio, Nicola Perrotti, and Cesare Musatti, who would later train almost all the other Italian psychoanalysts.

Bernhard encouraged his patients to let themselves go, to surrender, a message which was the central tenet of his teaching philosophy and of his therapeutic process. Consequently, he came to consider the book by the French Jesuit Jean-Pierre de Caussade, *Surrendering to Divine Providence*, to be of paramount importance. He later published it in the collection *Psyche and Conscience*, which he edited for the publisher Ubaldini. "His religion was an amalgam of Judaism, Christianity, and Buddhism, which emphasized the sense of a greater design within which we all move."[8]

In 1977, when Aldo Carotenuto published *Jung and Italian Culture* (for the same collection as the one edited by Bernhard), he was a young but already influential psychoanalyst. In one chapter of his book, he sketched an enlightening portrait of Federico Fellini that helps us understand the self-analytical value of *8 ½*.

"The film director and I," Carotenuto writes, "discussed at length his relationship with Bernhard. [Encountering Bernhard] was an extremely important event in Fellini's life. Their encounter took place in what could be called an exceptional time. It was somehow right that it happened—in general, certain encounters seem destined to take place. Very simple but, looking back at it, quite unexpected. Fellini was not well. He could define his malaise only vaguely: it was certainly existential but some of his 'bruises' were more than just neurotic. It was 1960/61 and right after *La Dolce Vita.* He had some quasi-mystical experiences which took place when he was a child, except that at the time he

kammer; meine Mutter hat sich jämmerlicherweise in Paris das Leben genommen. Daß ich selbst nicht aus dem Lager entfernt und nach Polen deportiert wurde, verdanke ich dem berühmten italienischen Orientalisten Tucci, der durch einige Patienten von mir gehört hatte und meine Entlassung bewirkte. Der Traum sagte es genau voraus: ein Italiener mit indisch anmutendem Gesicht."[7]

Nach dem Krieg nahm Bernhard seine Tätigkeit als Psychotherapeut wieder auf und sammelte eine Reihe von Wissenschaftlern um sich, unter denen sich Emilio Servadio, Nicola Perrotti und Cesare Musatti befanden, welche in der Folge fast alle anderen italienischen Psychoanalytiker ausbildeten. Bernhard empfahl seinen Patienten, sich gehen zu lassen, sich hinzugeben, diese Theorie stand im Mittelpunkt seiner Lehre und seiner Therapie. Daher schätzte er das Buch des französischen Jesuiten Jean-Pierre de Caussade *Hingabe an Gottes Vorsehung* besonders und publizierte es in der von ihm herausgegebenen Reihe *Psiche e coscienza* bei Ubaldini. „Seine Religion war eine Mischung aus Judentum, Christentum und Buddhismus, in der der Sinn für ein weiter gefaßtes Weltbild, in dem sich jeder Mensch bewegen sollte, besonders stark ausgeprägt war."[8]

Als Aldo Carotenuto 1977 in der von Bernhard herausgegebenen Reihe das Buch *Jung e la cultura italiana* veröffentlichte, war dieser, obwohl noch jung, bereits ein bedeutender Psychoanalytiker. In einem Kapitel des genannten Buches zeichnet Carotenuto ein erhellendes Porträt von Federico Fellini, das in erster Linie den autoanalytischen Wert von *8 ½* zu verstehen hilft.

„Wir haben," so schreibt Carotenuto, „lange mit dem Regisseur über dessen Verhältnis zu Bernhard gesprochen. [...] Dieses Verhältnis war ein extrem wichtiges Element in Fellinis Leben. Ihre Begegnung erfolgte sozusagen in einem Klima von Außergewöhnlichkeit. So wie es wohl kommen mußte und wie sich gewisse Begegnungen notwendigerweise entwickeln. Sehr einfach, aber auch sehr unerwartet. Dem Regisseur ging es nicht gut, ein Unwohlsein, welches er nur vage definieren konnte; existentiell, ja, aber mit „Ausbeulungen", die mehr als nur neurotisch waren. Es war um 1960/61, also nach *La Dolce Vita.* Ihm widerfuhren experimentelle Phänomene, die ihn schon als Kind heimgesucht hatten, nur daß er damals dachte, sie wären normal – und vielleicht waren sie es im Grunde auch. Fellini behauptete, diese Phänomene widerführen allen Men-thought these phenomena were normal—and maybe they are normal after all. Fellini believed that these moments happen to everyone, except that people bury them, put up such strong intellectual barriers that these experiences are subsumed and forgotten. But Fellini remembered them. As a result of nervous tension, or simply because it was meant to be, these strange phenomena reappeared in Fellini's life around the age of thirty-three or thirty-four. Experiences occurred that were not exactly within the realm of everyday normality, enhanced when he discovered an interest in the magical aspects of certain books. Actually, reading certain rare texts of initiates, prophets, and magicians with his avid and uncontrolled curiosity only stimulated in Fellini a natural tendency, an openness to these phenomena. Furthermore, Fellini's profession and his way of living within the sphere of the imagination further heightened his potential for hallucinatory experiences. This created in him a shift to a borderline condition in which sensibility was transformed into rather hypersensitized perception. On the one hand, he was tempted to let himself go, and go beyond, but on the other he shrank from the danger that this entailed. He was truly afraid. Had he not been gripped by a feeling of terror when he encountered these fascinating but totally unknown phenomena, things would probably have progressed even further. Instead, he was held back by a real fear that he could not control.

One day, when he felt himself waver after one of these encounters—which had left him feeling very pleased and alarmed at the same time—a friend with whom he had a work-related friendship dropped in to see him. Fellini had not seen this friend for a while. He had unsuccessfully tried to help him complete a movie that had remained unfinished due to a lack of money. Fellini was sure that De Seta harbored a grudge against him but, on the contrary, the former had gone to Fellini's house to tell him he had managed to finish his documentary—and to thank him for trying to help. Suddenly De Seta asked him: "Do you know Dr. Bernhard?" Fellini answered that he did not. "He is an extraordinary man. A psychoanalyst. I am very grateful to him. We talked about you the other day, about *La Strada*. Why don't you call him?" Now,

schen, sie vergäßen es aber und bauten eine intellektuelle Barriere auf, so daß die Angelegenheit erlosch und verschwand. Fellini hingegen erinnerte sich daran. Nach einer Zeit nervöser Spannungen, verschiedener Ereignisse oder vielleicht einfach, weil es so kommen mußte, sind bei ihm im Alter von 33 bis 34 Jahren erneut seltsame Phänomene aufgetreten, die vielleicht nicht dem üblichen Alltagsstreß zuzuschreiben waren. Diese wurden in der Folge mit der Entdeckung eines magischen Interesses für bestimmte Bücher noch verstärkt. In der Tat stürzte sich Fellini mit einer kaum kontrollierten und ein wenig lüsternen Neugierde auf die Lektüre der seltenen Texte von Eingeweihten, Propheten und Illusionisten, was seine natürliche Neigung und Offenheit für diese Dinge noch verstärkte. Darüber hinaus hat sein Beruf – das Leben in einer Sphäre der Imagination – wohl die Begeisterung über die Möglichkeiten verstärkt, halluzinatorische Aspekte auszuleben. Es war eine Gratwanderung, in der die normale Sensibilität zu einer beunruhigenden Wahrnehmung wird. Auf der einen Seite wollte er sich gehen lassen, wollte tiefer eindringen, auf der anderen Seite spürte er die Gefahr und bekam Angst. Wenn er nicht angesichts dieser faszinierenden, aber völlig unbekannten Phänomene den Schrecken gespürt hätte, hätte sich das Ganze wahrscheinlich noch weiter verschärft. Er wurde jedoch von einem authentischen Angstgefühl zurückgehalten, das er nicht zu kontrollieren vermochte.

Eines Tages, als er in Folge dieser Anfälle fast aus dem Gleichgewicht gekommen war – was ihn einerseits freute, andererseits aber auch erschreckte –, besuchte ihn ein Kollege, mit dem er beruflich nur selten zu tun hatte. Fellini hatte ihn länger nicht gesehen, genau gesagt, seit der Zeit nicht mehr, als Fellini vergeblich versucht hatte, ihn bei der Vollendung eines Films finanziell zu unterstützen. Daher fürchtete Fellini, sein Kollege würde ihm diese Geschichte noch nachtragen; anscheinend besuchte dieser ihn jedoch, um zu erzählen, daß er seinen Dokumentarfilm doch noch abgeschlossen hatte und auch um Fellini für seine Bemühungen zu danken. Dann fragte er plötzlich: „Kennst Du Dr. Bernhard?" Fellini verneinte die Frage. „Er ist ein außergewöhnlicher Mann. Ein Psychoanalytiker, dem ich viel zu verdanken habe. Kürzlich haben wir über Dich, d. h. über den Film *La Strada* gesprochen. Warum rufst Du ihn nicht einmal an?" Das Gespräch entwickelte sich natürlich rein zufällig in diese Richall this was completely arbitrary, especially since the friend knew nothing of what Fellini was going through. He left Fellini the doctor's number, and Fellini took it, out of courtesy but with no intention of using it, because he had had a past psychoanalytical experience that had been anything but positive [. . .]. Fellini's pockets were always full of scraps of paper on which various notes were written, and one day he found a piece of paper with just this number on it and nothing else. Thinking that it was the number of a woman he had met, he telephoned rather cautiously, for he did not want to let on that he did not know whom he was calling. When he heard the deep calm voice of a man at the other end of the line saying "Hello," Fellini asked: "Is Maria there?" "No, I'm sorry, there is no Maria here," Bernhard answered with his characteristic German accent. "Who is speaking?" Fellini asked, and the reply was: "Professor Bernhard." "Oh, I'm sorry Professor . . . you know . . . this is Fellini"; "Ah, yes, how do you do, what can I do for you?" There was a long silence and then, to get over his embarrassment, Fellini suddenly said: "I must speak to you." But it was not exactly true. He had simply not known how to end a phone call that had begun with quite different intentions.

And so Fellini went to speak to Bernhard. The man who came to the door looked like an Oriental master. Fellini liked everything about his house: the narrow corridor like the labyrinths of certain amusement parks, the sense of peace he found inside the doctor's studio. He could breathe in the spirituality there; it actually filled the room. They sat facing each other. Bernhard smiled. "What do you want to speak to me about?" And Fellini answered, "I have nothing to say. I feel that I am in front of a person who inspires me with a great sense of peace." "Do you know what I do? What I am?" Bernhard asked. "Yes, a psychoanalyst," Fellini answered, and then he spoke of *La Strada.* At the end, Fellini asked if he could come back to see him and Bernhard said: "Yes, whenever you want."

But Fellini did not call him for a long time, because, he said, he did not want to confront his anguish once more. And then one day, driven not so much by his neurotic malaise as by the desire to see Bernhard again, Fellini did call. Bernhard rec-

tung, zumal der Freund nicht wußte, was Fellini gerade durchmachte. Er ließ Fellini die Telefonnummer da. Um nicht unhöflich zu erscheinen, nahm Fellini sie an, dachte jedoch nicht im Geringsten daran anzurufen, zumal er mit der Psychoanalyse bereits eine eher unglückliche Erfahrung gemacht hatte. [...] Da Fellini die Angewohnheit besaß, viele Zettel mit unterschiedlichen Notizen in der Tasche zu haben, fand er eines Tages ein Stück Papier mit nichts anderem als der besagten Nummer darauf. Da er dachte, es handelte sich um die Nummer einer Frau, die er einmal kennengelernt hatte, telefonierte er mit einer gewissen Vorsicht, um sich nicht anmerken zu lassen, daß er nicht sicher war, bei wem er anrief. Am anderen Ende der Leitung hörte er die ruhige, tiefe Stimme eines Mannes, die Hallo" sagte, woraufhin Fellini fragte: „Ist Maria da?" „Nein, es tut mir leid, hier gibt es keine Maria", antwortete man ihm mit deutschem Akzent. „Aber wer spricht denn dort?" fragte Fellini. „Professor Bernhard". „Ach Herr Professor, entschuldigen Sie ... Wissen Sie ... ich bin Fellini." „Ach so, erfreut, was kann ich für Sie tun?" Es trat eine kurze Pause ein, die Fellini überstürzt beendete, um die peinliche Situation zu überbrücken. Er sagte: „Ich muß mit Ihnen sprechen", was er gar nicht vorgehabt hatte, er wußte nur nicht, wie er dieses nicht beabsichtigte Gespräch beenden sollte.

Er ging also zu Bernhard. Es öffnete ein Herr, der wie ein orientalischer Meister aussah. Alles in der Wohnung gefiel Fellini: der enge Flur, der ihn ein wenig an bestimmte Kirmes-Labyrinthe erinnerte, die Ruhe in seiner Praxis. Man konnte die Spiritualität förmlich einatmen, sie war im Raum. Die beiden setzten sich einander gegenüber, Bernhard lächelte und sagte: „Bitte", worauf Fellini antwortete: „Ich habe nichts zu sagen, mir kommt es vor, einer Person gegenüberzusitzen, die eine große Ruhe ausstrahlt." „Wissen Sie, was ich mache? Wer ich bin?" „Ja, Sie sind Psychoanalytiker." Dann sprach Fellini von *La Strada.* Zum Schluß fragte er, ob er wiederkommen dürfe, und Bernhard antwortete: „Ja, wann immer Sie wollen."

Fellini meldete sich lange Zeit nicht, er wußte nicht recht, was er tun sollte, und die alte Sache mit seinen Ängsten wollte er nicht wieder aufrollen. Dann aber rief er Bernhard eines Tages doch an, weniger wegen neurotischer Probleme, sondern einfach, weil er ihn wiedersehen wollte. Bernhard erkannte seine Stimme sofort, und sie verabredeten sich für eine halbe ognized him instantly and gave him an appointment an hour and a half hour later. From then on, he saw him very often, punctually, week after week. When Fellini talked to him about parapsychological phenomena, Bernhard would listen with great interest and then say smiling: "You realize, of course, that we have to see all this from the psychological point of view," somewhat disappointing Fellini, who would rather have continued seeing the whole thing from a magical perspective.

As he progressed, however, Fellini really felt that Bernhard was the right person for him, the friend and mentor he needed. They formed a relationship based on friendship and complete trust, to such a degree that we can say, from the existential and ideological, rather than the narrative points of view, that *8 ½* and *Juliet of the Spirits* were born from this encounter. Even though the director had already planned these stories, his encounter with Bernhard and with Jung's writings shed light upon aspects of them that he had not previously noticed.

But getting back to Bernhard, Fellini remembered a dream he had shortly before the former died. He dreamed that Bernhard had died, and Fellini had gone to offer his condolences. He knocked at the door of his beloved mentor's house and a mournful and languid young man appeared. He led him down a corridor to the studio where Bernhard lay on the floor, dead, wrapped like a mummy. As the dream continued, the vision of this cadaver disappeared and Fellini felt Bernhard's hands squeezing his wrists hard, almost as if to tell him he was not dead, that though invisible he could still communicate with him. He woke up in distress, uncertain whether to tell Bernhard his dream or not. He called to see how Bernhard was and went to see him soon afterwards. Once there he rather recklessly told Bernhard about the dream. The latter was not disturbed but became very serious and said nothing. Some time passed. Fellini returned to his work, and he and Bernhard even went to dinner together a couple of times. Fellini was shooting *Juliet of the Spirits* and wanted to show the film to him; Bernhard answered that he would like to see it very much. One day Fellini was working on the movie when a friend called to tell him of Bernhard's death. He stopped working immediate-

Stunde später. Von diesem Moment an sahen sie sich sehr oft, pünktlich und regelmäßig einmal die Woche. Als Fellini ihm von seinen parapsychologischen Phänomenen erzählte, hörte Bernhard mit großem Interesse zu und sagte dann lächelnd: „Sie verstehen, daß wir dies alles unter dem psychologischen Aspekt betrachten müssen", womit er Fellini ein wenig enttäuschte, weil dieser die Sache gern weiterhin in einem magischen Licht gesehen hätte.

Je länger die Therapie dauerte, desto mehr spürte Fellini, daß Bernhard genau die richtige Person war, der Freund, der Meister, den er brauchte. So entstand ein freundschaftliches Verhältnis mit tiefem Vertrauen, und man kann sagen, daß sowohl *8 ½* als auch *Julia und die Geister* im Kielwasser dieser Begegnungen entstanden sind, nicht so sehr bezüglich einer narrativen Notwenigkeit, es ging vielmehr um die existentielle, ideologische Note. Wenn auch der Handlungsrahmen der Filme bereits im Kopf des Regisseurs herumschwirrte, so beleuchteten die Begegnung mit Bernhard und die Lektüre der Texte von Jung einen Aspekt, den Fellini zuvor nicht gesehen hatte. [...]

Fellini erinnerte sich an einen Traum über Bernhard, den er kurz vor dessen Tod hatte. Er träumte, Bernhard sei gestorben. Fellini ging daraufhin los, um sein Beileid auszusprechen. Er klingelte an der Tür seines geliebten Meisters, und es öffnete ein junger Mann mit einem matten Gesichtsausdruck voller Trauer; dieser schritt vor Fellini den Flur entlang, und sie gelangten in das Zimmer, in dem der tote Bernhard wie eine Mumie eingewickelt am Boden lag. Im weiteren Verlauf des Traums verschwand das Bild der Leiche, und Fellini spürte, wie seine Handgelenke fest von Bernhards Händen ergriffen wurden. Dadurch wurde ihm suggeriert, Bernhard sei nicht tot, er sei auch unsichtbar anwesend. Fellini erwachte verwirrt und war sich nicht sicher, ob er Bernhard den Traum erzählen sollte. Er rief ihn an, um zu hören, wie es ihm ging, und besuchte ihn kurz darauf. Einmal dort, erzählte Fellini ihm vielleicht übereilt von seinem Traum. Bernhard ließ sich nicht verwirren, wurde aber sehr ernst und sagte nichts dazu. Es verging einige Zeit. Fellini nahm seine Arbeit wieder auf, mehrmals gingen die beiden sogar zusammen essen. Fellini drehte gerade *Julia und die Geister* und wollte Bernhard den Film zeigen. Er erzählte ihm davon und Bernhard antwortete, daß er den Film gern sehen würde. Eines Tages, als Fellini gerade an dem ly and ran to Bernhard's house, only to find the man from his dream answer the door. Seeing him there upset Fellini very much. The man led him down the corridor and then very delicately went away, leaving him alone with Bernhard. The director thought that the second part of his dream was going to come true and was so frightened that he begged Bernhard not to move, not to take him by the wrists. He doubted that Bernhard was really dead. Afterwards he dreamed about him again, but always in a very happy and clownish way, as a surprising presence. Their relationship was unquestionably one of the most important experiences of Fellini's life. He had been Fellini's father in a very real sense."[9]

Bernhard, then, had become a true father to Fellini, the one who gave him the internal support to realize his masterpiece. Like all masterpieces, *8 ½* elicited both great enthusiasm and profound aversion when it was released. The most intellectually penetrating of all the critiques was written by Mario Verdone for *Bianco e Nero*. Verdone wrote: "For a man so often accused of histrionics and insincerity, in this autobiographical work we are faced with the 'moment of truth' of a kind that we have never seen before. Fellini is trying to look within himself: he is X-raying his own creative process, psychoanalyzing himself. He transfigures his own internal emotions in the attempt to 'free himself.' He tells the story of his intimate vertigo, after a creative effort that had arrested him, almost totally blocking his path so that he had to flee to his Marienbad 'from the air' because there were no other escape routes. The work is a brilliant improvisation—even though organizing it at the logical and psychological levels was no easy task. Feigning improvisation has never demanded so much work and meditation as it does in the movies, and especially in a movie like this. In it Fellini has outlined the arabesque of his particular spiritual condition. The work becomes the most difficult game of skill that the director has ever taken on. It is like a series of acrobatic feats that a tightrope walker performs above the crowd, apparently agile, smooth, and in a state of grace, always at the point of making a more dangerous and more amazing jump and at the same time of falling and crashing to the ground.

Film arbeitete, klingelte das Telefon, und ein Freund informierte ihn über Bernhards Tod. Fellini unterbrach die Arbeit, fuhr zu Bernhards Haus, und der junge Mann aus dem Traum öffnete ihm die Tür. Als Fellini den Mann sah, fühlte er, wie die Angst in ihm hochstieg. Der Mann ging vor ihm her durch den Flur, entfernte sich dann aber diskret, so daß Fellini mit Bernhard allein war. Der Regisseur dachte, nun würde sich auch der zweite Teil des Traums verwirklichen, und hatte Angst. Er war sicher, Bernhard wäre noch nicht tot und bat ihn mit kindlichem Flehen liegen zu bleiben und nicht seine Handgelenke zu umfassen. Fellini träumte noch öfter von Bernhard. Es waren aber immer sehr heitere, lustige Träume, die ihn überraschend anwesend sein ließen. Ohne Zweifel war das Verhältnis der beiden eine der wichtigsten Erfahrungen im Leben Fellinis. Bernhard war für ihn eine Vaterfigur."[9]

Bernhard war für Fellini also wie ein Vater, derjenige, der ihm den inneren Halt gab, um sein Werk zu verwirklichen. Ein Meisterwerk, welches – wie alle wahren Meisterwerke – bei seiner Veröffentlichung neben enthusiastischem Lob auch große Ablehnung erfuhr. Die glänzendste Kritik schrieb sicherlich Mario Verdone in der Filmzeitschrift *Bianco e Nero*: „Für einen Menschen, der so oft des Komödiantentums und der Unaufrichtigkeit beschuldigt wird, glaube ich, daß es sich – bei diesem autobiographischen Werk – um die Stunde der Wahrheit handelt, wie es sie zuvor vielleicht noch nicht gegeben hat. Fellini versucht, in sich selbst zu lesen: er durchleuchtet den eigenen kreativen Prozeß, er analysiert sich mit dem Ziel der Befreiung, er verwandelt seine Emotionen, erzählt von seinem inneren Schwindel infolge einer kreativen Anstrengung, der dem Regisseur derart den Weg verbaut, daß dieser sich gezwungen sieht, in „Richtung Himmel", da es doch sonst keinen anderen Ausweg gibt, in Richtung seines Marienbads zu flüchten. [...] Das Werk präsentiert sich als geniale Improvisation, obwohl dessen Organisation auf logischer und psychologischer Ebene sicherlich nicht einfach gewesen ist. Denn Kino, insbesondere ein solcher Film, bedarf großer Anstrengung und viel Nachdenkens, um die Fiktion der Improvisation aufrecht zu erhalten. Fellini hat darin die Arabesken einer bestimmten Geisteshaltung nachgezeichnet. Der Film ist zu dem schwierigsten Geschicklichkeitsspiel geworden, dem sich der Regisseur jemals gestellt hat. *8 ½* erscheint wie eine Reihe akrobatischer Kunststücke, die

But the acrobat somehow knows how to perform the right somersault at the right time. With a leap he straightens up, is saved, and triumphs. For the public who is watching this singular, surprising, anxiety-provoking, and alarming spectacle to the very end, there is nothing left to do but applaud. The exercise has been successfully completed."[10]

As everyone knows, the movie tells the story of a famous director who cannot start his new movie because of the many nightmares, childhood memories, and feelings of guilt that ensnare him. But, in the end, the film begins in a fascinating circuslike atmosphere.

Inevitably so, because in following Bernhard's teachings, Fellini could do nothing other than let it begin. "I can be interested in describing chaos," he said, "only if I see a way out of the chaos; otherwise, I would feel that I am narrowing in a dishonest way. Maybe this is a limitation of mine, but at the same time, I feel it is a test of an artist's vitality. I don't think the film could have existed or could have made any sense without this ending."[11]

As the crowning achievement of the entire cinematic event, the finale of *8 ½* (inevitably) contains all the gaiety that reigned on the set during the weeks in which the movie was being shot; the vital impulse that the author rediscovered after looking inside himself. All who took part in *8 ½* remember this magical atmosphere, so masterfully captured by the photographer Tazio Secchiaroli. The photographer recalled: "I felt that the central character of the film was Fellini himself." Secchiaroli's feeling, totally instinctive, came from his own natural ability to capture psychological nuances.

This capacity also endowed him with the ability to somehow foresee events and to elicit his subjects' most intimate character from the ever-changing facets of their expressions and attitudes. Arriving on that magical set, the photographer therefore provided the final piece of the fortunate puzzle of people and events that created the twentieth-century myth of *8 ½*.

ein Seiltänzer nach außen hin locker, gelöst und grazil oberhalb der Menge durchführt, obgleich immer kurz vor dem gefährlichsten und gleichzeitig wundersamsten Sprung, immer unmittelbar vor dem Fall, der seinen Körper am Boden zerschmettern würde. Aber der Akrobat meistert im passenden Augenblick den richtigen Überschlag, und plötzlich steht er wieder, hat sich gerettet und gewonnen. Der Zuschauer, der diesem einzigartigen Spektakel voller Überraschungen mit Besorgnis und Unruhe beiwohnt, kann am Schluß nur applaudieren. Die Übung ist gelungen."[10]

Bekanntlich erzählt der Film die Geschichte eines berühmten Regisseurs, dem es – von vielen Alpträumen, Kindheitserinnerungen und Schuldgefühlen geplagt – nicht gelingt, mit seinem neuen Film anzufangen. Erst am Ende beginnen die Dreharbeiten in einer faszinierenden Zirkusatmosphäre.

Unvermeidlich, denn – Bernhard zufolge – kann Fellini nichts anderes tun, als mit den Dreharbeiten beginnen: „Mich", so sagt er, „kann es nur interessieren, das Chaos zu beschreiben, wenn ich aus diesem Chaos einen Ausweg sehe; andernfalls schiene es mir, den Film auf unredliche Weise enden zu lassen. Dies ist vielleicht meine eigene Grenze, meiner Meinung nach belegt es aber die Vitalität eines Autors. Ich glaube nicht, daß der Film ohne dieses Finale möglich gewesen wäre oder einen Sinn gehabt hätte."[11]

Die Freude im Finale von *8 ½*, die auch während der wochenlangen Dreharbeiten auf dem Set herrschte, der vitale Schwung, den der Autor wiederfindet, nachdem er tief in sein Inneres geschaut hat, krönt unweigerlich die gesamte Produktion des Films. Alle Beteiligten erinnern sich an diese zauberhafte Atmosphäre, welche Tazio Secchiaroli so meisterlich festgehalten hat. „Ich spürte", erinnert sich der Fotograf, „daß die Hauptperson des Films Fellini war."

Dieses instinktive Gefühl Secchiarolis entstand aus seiner natürlichen Fähigkeit, psychologische Nuancen zu erkennen. Er besaß mit dieser Fähigkeit einen sechsten Sinn, der es ihm ermöglichte, in gewisser Weise die Ereignisse vorauszusehen, und aus den veränderlichen Falten der Mimik und Gestik der von ihm Fotografierten deren innerste Natur nach außen zu kehren.

Mit seiner Anwesenheit am Set vervollständigte der Fotograf die glückliche Verflechtung von Ereignissen und Personen, die den Jahrhundertmythos von *8 ½* ausmachen sollten.

Tazio Secchiaroli

Tazio Secchiaroli was born on November 26, 1925, in Centocelle, then a cluster of houses in the middle of the Roman countryside. His family was originally from an area known as the Marches, on the Adriatic Sea west of Umbria and Tuscany. His father was the son of a farmer who traveled to Rome in winter in order to work in the vegetable gardens that still surrounded the city at the time.

The distance from Centocelle to the center of Rome was only ten kilometers, a train ride on the Rome-Frosinone line of less than half an hour. But for the inhabitants of this periphery—now the greater metropolitan region—the psychological distance was enormous. In fact, they saw themselves as neither Romans nor villagers, a feeling that clearly illustrates the force it took back in 1930, for young men like Secchiaroli to try in various ways to make it in the city—and, often, to succeed.

On the afternoon of April 27, 1937, construction began on Cinecittà, the great film studio being erected not far from Centocelle. Tazio Secchiaroli was twelve years old at the time. He never imagined that the area—inaugurated by Mussolini himself in an official ceremony with Fascist party leaders, flags, fanfare, and uniformed children—would someday become his second home. Secchiaroli first set foot in this "city of cinema" in 1943, working as a messenger boy. There was no gasoline during the war and famous actors like Alida Valli, Amedeo Nazzari, Luisa Ferida, and Osvaldo Valenti had to travel to and from Cinecittà with the commoners, on the train linking Rome with the surrounding hilltowns.

After a few months, Secchiaroli quit his job. He also never imagined that his return to the "nine sheds surrounded by a wall" would not mean the short route through the six kilometers of countryside that separate Centocelle from Cinecittà, but instead involve a much longer journey that would take him fifteen years. What intervened was a rite of passage that led him through Via Veneto and the events of the summer of 1958.

He had already taken his first photographs in 1941, from the side lines of a soccer field using a friend's

Tazio Secchiaroli

Geboren wurde Tazio Secchiaroli am 26. November 1925 in Centocelle, einem Ort, der damals aus ein paar Häusern inmitten der römischen Campagna bestand. Secchiarolis Familie stammte aus den Marken. Sein Vater war der Sohn von Bauern, die im Winter nach Rom kamen, um in den Gemüsegärten zu arbeiten, die die Stadt zu dieser Zeit noch umgaben. Von Centocelle bis ins Zentrum von Rom waren es weniger als zehn Kilometer, für die Strecke brauchte man mit dem Bummelzug Rom–Frosinone etwa eine halbe Stunde. Aber für die Bewohner des kleinen Ortes, der heute ein Stadtteil von Rom innerhalb der Peripherie ist, war die Entfernung psychologisch riesig. Sie fühlten sich in der Tat weder als richtige Städter noch als Landbewohner. Daraus erklärt sich die Vehemenz, mit der einige, die wie Secchiaroli in den 30er Jahren aufgewachsen sind, auf unterschiedliche Weise die Stadt erobern wollten, was ihnen häufig auch gelang.

Wenig später, am Nachmittag des 27. April 1937, wurden die Studios von Cinecittà aus der Taufe gehoben. Tazio war damals gerade 12 Jahre alt und konnte sich nicht vorstellen, daß dieser Ort, der von Mussolini persönlich in einem Festakt mit politischen Würdenträgern, Fahnen, Fanfaren und Kindern in Uniform eingeweiht wurde, für ihn zu einem zweiten Zuhause werden würde.

Diese „Stadt des Kinos" betrat Secchiaroli erstmals im Kriegsjahr 1943, und zwar als Laufbursche. Benzin war in dieser Zeit knapp, und so waren selbst so berühmte Schauspieler wie Alida Valli, Amedeo Nazzari, Luisa Ferida und Osvaldo Valenti dazu gezwungen, wie alle anderen auch, nach Cinecittà den Zug von Rom zu den Castelli zu nehmen. Als er seinen Job dort nach einigen Monaten aufgab, konnte er sich wohl kaum vorstellen, daß er, um in diese „neun von einer Mauer umgebenen Hallen" zurückzukehren, nicht nur die sechs Kilometer Landstraße, sondern einen sehr viel weiteren Weg zurücklegen mußte, der ganze 15 Jahre in Anspruch nehmen sollte. Er konnte natürlich nicht wissen, daß ihn sein Weg zurück über die Via Veneto und die Ereignisse des Sommers '58 führen würde.

Bereits 1941 machte er mit der Kodak Retina 35 mm eines seiner Freunde am Rand eines Fußballfelds bei Centocelle seine ersten Fotos. Die Vorstellung, „die

35mm Kodak Retina. The idea of "capturing things" with that small box fascinated him. So in 1944 when he left his job as a messenger at Cinecittà, he struck out to make a living working as a street photographer. He became one of the many itinerant photographers who circulated in Rome, around the train stations and the most important monuments, taking photographs of American soldiers and of the usual tourists, moving in summer to the beaches of Ostia where (especially on Saturday and Sunday), they snapped photographs of children, couples, and families feasting on watermelon. His earnings never exceeded the level of pure survival. This is how Tazio Secchiaroli lived his first five years as a professional photographer—until 1951.

His first turning point occurred in 1952, when he began to freelance for the Vedo agency. "At the time," Secchiaroli said, "Vedo was an old, rundown photo agency. But it was still an important experience for me, because it allowed me to meet an extraordinary figure, to listen to his stories, and to see his photographs: it was a real stroke of luck for me." He was speaking of the agency's founder, the legendary Adolfo Porry-Pastorel, one of the fathers of Italian photojournalism. "This person," Secchariaroli wrote, "left a mark in me that analysts call 'imprinting.'" What Secchiaroli meant by imprinting becomes apparent from a conversation that the photographer had with students of the Instituto di Scienze dello Spettacolo (Institute of Performance Arts) of the University of Rome in 1983: "In his time, Porry was considered to be a very devious person and his colleagues were afraid of him, because he would play dirty tricks on them like sticking stamps on their lenses. (There were no reflex cameras with direct vision then, so you didn't look directly through the lens and you wouldn't notice immediately if there was anything covering it.) Pastorel often used these rather unorthodox methods, sometimes to get an exclusive, which is why he was not very well liked."

In order to get to know Porry-Pastorel better, Secchiaroli made the journey to see him on Sundays at Castel San Pietro, the small town where Porry lived (and of which he was the mayor). Once he even spent an entire week of his vacation there,

Dinge einzufangen", faszinierte ihn. So versuchte er 1944, nachdem er seinen Job als Laufbursche in Cinecittà verloren hatte, von der Fotografie zu leben, und wurde Straßenfotograf. Wie viele andere in Rom trieb er sich rund um den Bahnhof und in der Nähe der bedeutendsten Monumente herum, er fotografierte amerikanische Soldaten und die üblichen Touristen. Im Sommer verlagerte er seine Tätigkeit an die Strände von Ostia, wo er samstags und vor allem sonntags versuchte, Kinder, Liebespaare und Familien beim Melonenessen zu fotografieren. Der Verdienst sicherte dabei gerade mal das Überleben.

Auf diese Weise verbrachte Tazio Secchiaroli die ersten fünf Jahre seiner professionellen Tätigkeit, also bis 1951, als Fotograf.

Seinen ersten Scoop landete er 1952, als er anfing mit der Agentur VEDO zusammenzuarbeiten. „In dieser Zeit", so sagte er, „war die Agentur bereits veraltet und marode. Doch für mich war sie von außerordentlicher Bedeutung, weil ich dort die Möglichkeit hatte, einen ungewöhnlichen Menschen kennenzulernen, seine Geschichten zu hören und seine Fotos zu sehen: Für mich war das ein absoluter Glücksfall." Kennengelernt hat er den Gründer, den legendären Adolfo Porry-Pastorel, einen der Väter des italienischen Fotojournalismus.

„Diese Persönlichkeit", schreibt Tazio, „hat in mir eine Spur hinterlassen, die die Psychoanalytiker als Imprinting (Prägung) bezeichnen." Worin diese Prägung besteht, verdeutlicht eine Äußerung des Fotografen aus dem Jahr 1983 während eines Gesprächs mit Studenten der Theaterwissenschaften an der Universität von Rom: „Zu seiner Zeit galt Porry als absolut ‚gerissen', und seine Kollegen fürchteten ihn, weil er ihnen gerne böse Streiche spielte. Er klebte z. B. Briefmarken auf ihre Objektive. Damals gab es noch keine Reflexkameras, d. h. man schaute nicht direkt durch das Objektiv, bemerkte also nicht, wenn es von irgend etwas verdeckt wurde. Pastorel benutzte oft solch unlautere Praktiken, um zu einem Exklusivfoto zu kommen, und er war deshalb nicht eben besonders beliebt." Um Porry-Pastorel besser kennenzulernen, fuhr Secchiaroli an den Sonntagen oft nach Castel San Pietro, dem Dorf, in dem Porry lebte und Bürgermeister war. Einmal verbrachte er dort eine ganze Woche, um dem Mann zuzuhören, den er als seinen wahren Lehrmeister ansah. So kam so that he could devote more time to listening to the stories and teachings of the person he considered a maestro. In doing so he acquired some of Porry's shrewdness, his sense of timing, and his determination. Together these qualities made Secchiaroli one of the most famous photographers of the Via Veneto.

His celebrity began with a short article on the front page of the Milanese daily *Il Giorno* on Tuesday, August 19, 1958, entitled "Photographer Assaulted by Farouk and Franciosa." "A photographer," the article said, "lived through some dramatic moments on Friday night on the Via Veneto when he was first assaulted by an ex-king, Farouk of Egypt, and then by an actor, Anthony Franciosa. The story began at 2:00 am on August 15th, on the rive gauche, at the Café de Paris, whose clientele, the night-wandering social crowd, was greatly increased by the ex-sovereign's considerable bulk. . . ." Five days later (on August 24th), the weekly *L'Espresso* (one of the most authoritative magazines of the time) relaunched the news with a half-page article: "August 15th in Rome. The Terrible Night of Via Veneto." Two small news items, together with a series of protagonists that combined the past with the present, adding in a king, bodyguards, female companions, policemen, photoreporters, and show business people, became the stuff of legend.

In a very short time Secchiaroli became Italy's most famous photographer. That reputation was secured particularly after Federico Fellini's movie *La Dolce Vita* was released. The movie launched the legend of the Via Veneto and coined the word "paparazzo." It also marked the beginning of a friendship between Secchiaroli and Fellini and the occasion on which the photographer met Marcello Mastroianni, who, in turn, introduced him to Sophia Loren. The actress immediately recognized the extraordinary photographic talent of the boy from Centocelle and invited him to work for her.

Thus Secchiaroli became the personal photographer of the greatest star of Italian cinema in 1964, and, along with Sophia Loren, toured the world. Though he stood elbow to elbow with the screen's most famous actors and directors, he always maintained his signature simplicity, wise optimism, and easygoing, jovial gaiety. His relationship with the

es, daß er gewisse Züge von Porry übernahm, auch er war den anderen immer einen Schritt voraus und ließ sich durch nichts von einer Sache abbringen. Das machte ihn zum berühmtesten Fotografen der Via Veneto.

Sein Ruhm begann mit einer Pressenotiz auf der Titelseite der Mailänder Tageszeitung *Il Giorno* vom Dienstag, den 19. August 1958. Die Schlagzeile lautete „Fotograf von Faruk und Franciosa angegriffen". Und der Text führte aus: „Dramatische Ereignisse erlebte ein Fotograf Freitagnacht in der Via Veneto, als er zuerst von dem ehemaligen König Faruk von Ägypten und dann von dem Schauspieler Anthony Franciosa angegriffen wurde. Das ganze ereignete sich in der Nacht des 15. August ab zwei Uhr morgens im Café de Paris am linken Tiberufer. Jede Nacht füllten mehr mondäne Nachtschwärmer das Café und zu dieser Stunde auch die stattliche Erscheinung des ehemaligen Machthabers."

Fünf Tage später, am 24. August, erschien die Meldung in einer der damals einflußreichsten Wochenzeitschriften, dem *Espresso*, mit einem halbseitigen Artikel. Die Schlagzeile: „Der 15. August in Rom. Die schreckliche Nacht auf der Via Veneto". Zwei an sich unbedeutende Stories wurden so zu einem Mythos voller Figuren der Vergangenheit und Gegenwart: Könige, Leibwächter, Begleiterinnen, Polizisten, Fotoreporter und Schauspieler.

Innerhalb kürzester Zeit wurde Secchiaroli zum berühmtesten Fotografen Italiens. Dazu trug vor allem Federico Fellinis Film *La Dolce Vita* bei. Es war in der Tat dieser Film, der den Mythos der Via Veneto und den Begriff Paparazzo hervorbrachte. Der Film war der Anfang einer Freundschaft zwischen Secchiaroli und Fellini und führte zu der Begegnung mit Marcello Mastroianni, der wiederum den Fotografen Sophia Loren vorstellte. Die Schauspielerin erkannte das außergewöhnliche fotografische Talent des Jungen aus Centocelle und lud ihn sofort zur Zusammenarbeit ein.

So wurde Secchiaroli 1964 der persönliche Fotograf der größten Filmdiva des italienischen Kinos. Mit Sophia Loren hat Tazio die Welt bereist. Seite an Seite mit den berühmtesten Schauspielern und Regisseuren hat er doch immer seine Einfachheit bewahrt: mit seinem weisen Optimismus, mit seiner friedfertigen und heiteren Fröhlichkeit. Seine Verbindung mit der

actress was only interrupted by his decision to stop working. "Because," he said, "photography, like every art form, calls for great vital energy. In 1983, I felt that I no longer had that energy. So I decided to stop."
That decision is a testimony to Secchiaroli's sense of moderation, his awareness of the value of things, and above all his essential human decency. These qualities underlined the authentic modesty that accompanied him all the days of his life, until his untimely death on the night between the twenty-fourth and twenty-fifth of July 1998.

Schauspielerin endete erst, als er beschloß die Fotografie aufzugeben. „Denn", wie er sagt, „die Fotografie erfordert wie jede Kunst eine große Lebenskraft. 1983 spürte ich, daß diese Energie in mir erlosch. Und so beschloß ich aufzuhören."
In dieser Betrachtung zeigt sich Tazios ganzes Taktgefühl, sein Bewußtsein über die Bedeutung der Dinge, seine menschliche Zurückhaltung. Gefühle, die die Basis der authentischen Bescheidenheit bildeten, die ihn Tag für Tag begleitete, bis zu seinem verfrühten Tod in der Nacht vom 24. auf den 25. Juli 1998.

1 "Confessione in pubblico", Colloquium with Federico Fellini, in *Bianco e Nero* XXIV, April 4, 1963, p. 2.

2 Ibidem, p. 3.

3 Tullio Kezich, *Fellini*, Rizzoli, Milan, 1987, p. 301.

4 Ibidem, p. 303.

5 Aldo Carotenuto, *Jung e la cultura del XX secolo*, Bompiani, Milan, 1995, p. 121.

6 Ernst Bernhard, *Mitobiografia*, Adelphi, Milan, 1969, p. 7.

7 Ibidem, p. 8.

8 Aldo Carotenuto, *Jung e la cultura italiana*, Astrolabio – Ubaldini, Rome, 1977, p. 86.

9 Ibidem, pp. 137–142.

10 Mario Verdone, "L'ora della verità di un artista", in *Bianco e Nero* XXIV, April 1, 1963, pp. 50-53; now in Mario Verdone, *Federico Fellini*, Editrice Il Castoro, Milan, 1994.

11 "Confessione in pubblico", Colloquium with Federico Fellini, op. cit., p. 11.

1 „Confessione in pubblico", Gespräch mit Federico Fellini, in *Bianco e Nero*, XXIV, 4. April 1963, S. 2.

2 Idem, S. 3.

3 Tullio Kezich, *Fellini: eine Biographie*, Diogenes, Zürich 1989, S. 436

4 Idem, S. 303.

5 Aldo Carotenuto, *Jung e la cultura del XX secolo*, Bompiani, Mailand 1995, S. 121.

6 Ernst Bernhard: *Mytobiografia*, Adelphi, Mailand 1969, p. 7.

7 Idem, S. 8.

8 Aldo Carotenuto, *Jung e la cultura italiana*, Astrolabio – Ubaldini, Rom 1977, S. 86.

9 Idem, S. 137–142.

10 Mario Verdone: „L'ora della verità di un artista", in *Bianco e Nero*, XXIV, 4. April 1963, S. 50–53, auch in: Mario Verdone, *Federico Fellini*, Editrice Il Castoro, Mailand 1994.

11 „Confessione in pubblico", Gespräch mit Federico Fellini, op. cit., S. 11.

The Characters

Die Mitwirkenden

Federico Fellini
Film Director
Der Regisseur

Marcello Mastroianni
Guido Anselmi

Claudia Cardinale
Claudia

Anouk Aimée
Luisa

Sandra Milo
Carla

Edra Gale
Saraghina

Barbara Steele
Gloria

Giuditta Rissone
Guido's mother
Guidos Mutter

Elisabetta Catalano
Luisa's sister
Luisas Schwester

Guido's other women
Die anderen Frauen

Tazio Secchiaroli
The Photographer
Der Fotograf
(Photo: Gina Lollobrigida)

"Remember that this is a funny movie."
This reminder, attached to the camera, was Fellini's mantra throughout the making of the film.

„Denk daran, es soll ein komischer Film sein".
Dieses an die Kamera geheftete Motto begleitete Fellini während der gesamten Dreharbeiten.

ARTINI

“Well, the main problem is, your script lacks a fundamental idea.
It has no philosophic premise whatsoever.
The film is merely a series of completely senseless episodes.
Oh, their ambiguous realism is, perhaps, quite amusing . . .
but what is the writer's real intention?
To make us think? To frighten us?
From the very opening scenes,
there's a total lack of poetic inspiration.”

„Eins ist mir bei der Lektüre des Buchs sofort aufgefallen,
der Mangel an jeglicher Problematik oder, wenn Sie so wollen,
philosophischer Grundlage ... Das macht den Film
zu einer Folge von unzusammenhängenden Episoden.
Ich will durchaus nicht bestreiten, daß Sie sehr
unterhaltsam sein können in ihrem zweideutigen Realismus,
aber man fragt sich, was wollen sie eigentlich, die Autoren?
Wollen Sie uns zum Nachdenken anregen?
Oder wollen Sie uns Angst einjagen?...
Die Story enthüllt von Anfang bis Ende
eine solche Armut an dichterischen Einfällen.“

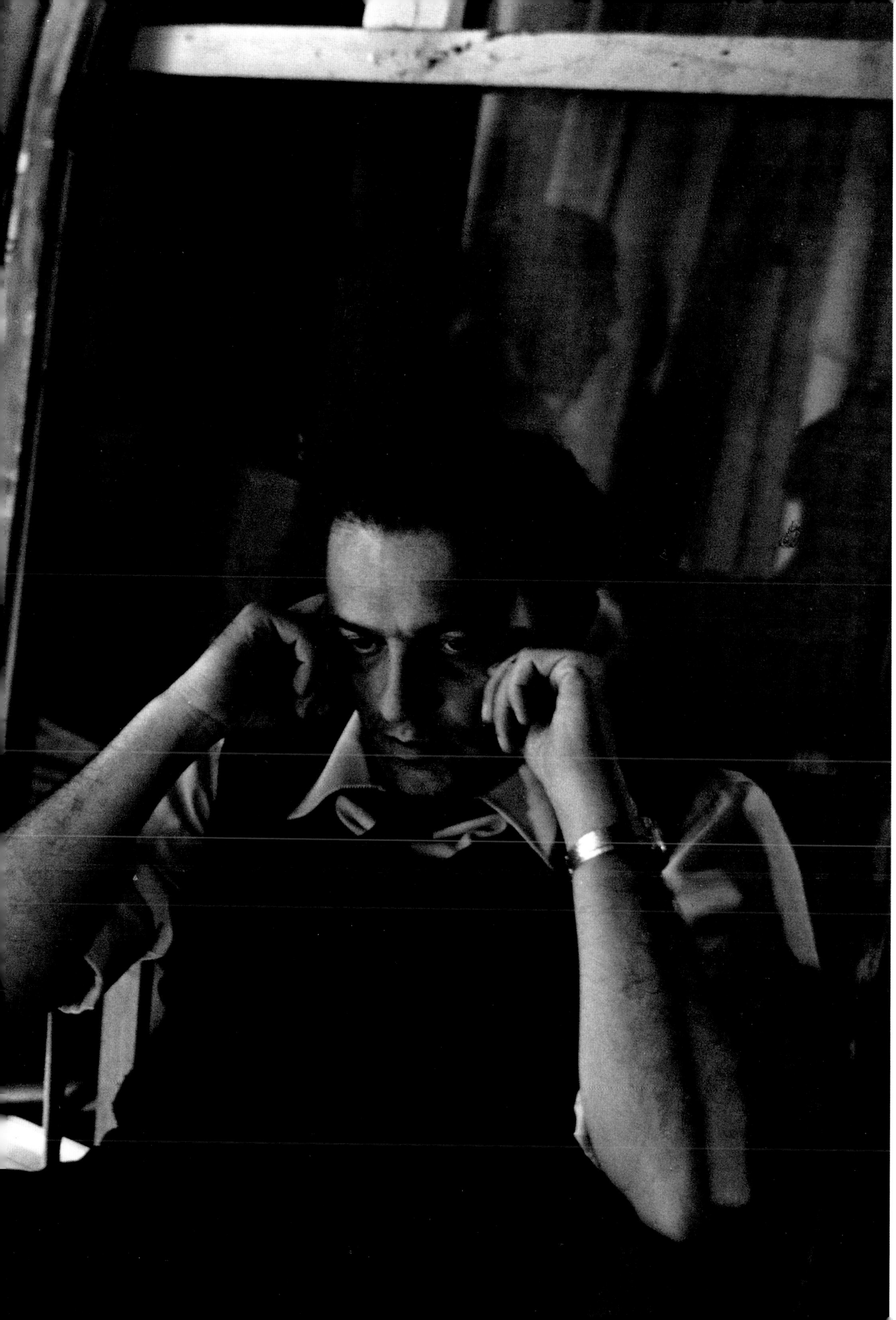

I thought I had everything clear in my mind. I wanted to make an honest film
. . . no lies, no compromises. I thought I had something so simple . . .
so simple to say. . . . No, I'm totally confused now. . .
Who knows why things turned out this way? Where did it all go wrong?
I really have nothing to say. But I want to say it just the same."

„Und ich glaubte, ich hätte so klare Vorstellungen,
ich wollte einen ehrlichen Film machen.
Ich glaubte, ich hätte etwas so Einfaches,
so leicht Verständliches zu sagen.
Und jetzt weiß ich nicht, wo mir der Kopf steht ...
Ich hab' heute einfach nichts zu sagen und doch will ich was sagen."

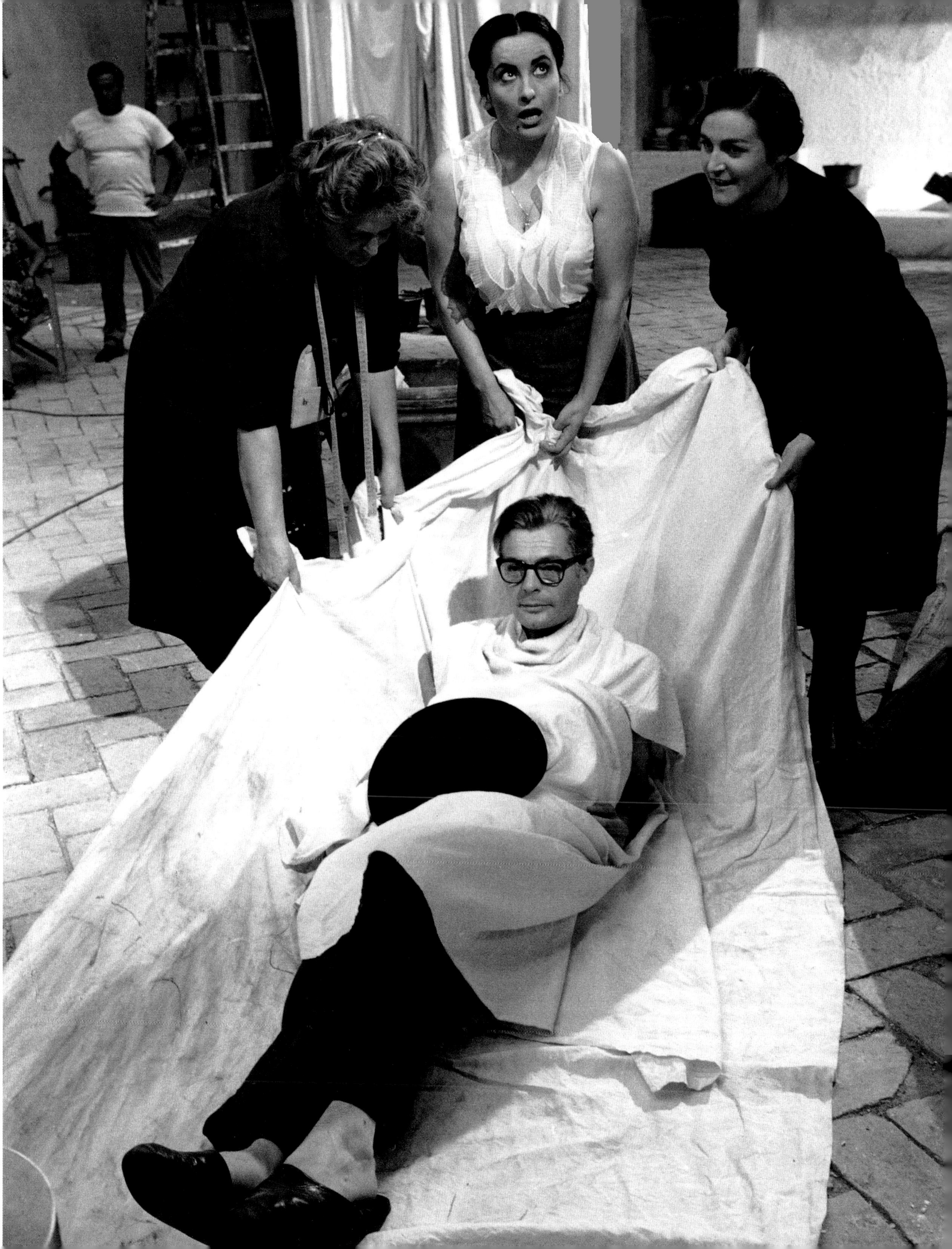

“I really don’t understand. This man meets a girl
who can be his salvation. But he rejects her.”
“Because he doesn’t believe it. . . .”
“Because he doesn’t know how to love.”
“Because no woman can change a man.”

„Ich verstehe das nicht, er begegnet einem Mädchen,
daß ihn retten könnte, und er weist sie zurück.“
„Weil er nicht mehr glauben kann,“
„... weil er nicht mehr lieben kann.“
„Ach, weil es nicht wahr ist,
daß eine Frau einen Mann ändern kann.“

The maestro. . . . The genius of improvisation! . . . Get away, you fool!
"No, it's a serious movie. . . . You are right. . . .
But I am sure that it has hit the mark . . . very sure."

„Der Meister! ... Das Improvisationsgenie! ... Geh, Du Narr!"
„Nein, es ist ein anspruchsvoller Film ... Du hast Recht ...
Aber ich bin sicher, daß er einschlägt ... Ganz bestimmt."

813 2
OPERATORE
G. DI VENANZO
FELLINI N 8½